Triceratops Up Close

Horned Dinosaur

Peter Dodson, PhD

Zoom In on Dinosaurs!

Illustrated by Bob Walters and Erin M. Cobb

CONTENTS

Words to Know

crest—A wide sheet of bone at the back of the head on horned dinosaurs. It is also called a frill.

dinosaur (DY noh sor)—Reptiles that lived from about 230 million years ago to 65 million years ago. They had a special kind of hip and long legs.

fossil (FAH sul)—Parts of living things from long ago. They are often turned to stone.

horn—A long bone with a sharp end. It grows out of the head.

possum (also called opossum)—A slow-moving mammal with a pouch for its young and a ratlike tail.

reptile (REP tyl)—Animals with scales that live on land and lay eggs. Dinosaurs, turtles, crocodiles, snakes, and lizards are reptiles.

Pronunciation Guide

Ankylosaurus [an KYE luh SOR us]

Chasmosaurus [KAZ muh SOR us]

Edmontosaurus [ed MONT uh SOR us]

Torosaurus [TOR uh SOR us]

Triceratops [try SAIR uh tops]

Plant Eater

Triceratops was a large, strong **dinosaur** that ate plants.

It walked on four legs.

Triceratops had three **horns** on its face. It looked a bit like a rhino. Its horns made it very dangerous.

The name *Triceratops* means "three-horned face."

Horns

Triceratops had one of the largest heads of any animal that ever lived on land.

The two horns over its eyes were three feet long.

A short horn sat over its nose.

The horns were used to scare off attackers.

The males used them to fight with other males.

Teeth and Beak

Triceratops had many teeth.

It had a thin beak at the front of its mouth. It used its beak to break open tough plants.

Triceratops ate plants that grew close to the ground.

It could reach bushes and low branches of trees.

Crest

Triceratops had a large, fan-shaped **crest.**

The crest was on the back of its head.

A male *Triceratops* used this crest to get a female *Triceratops* to notice him.

You can see how the size of *Triceratops* was almost the same as the size of a rhino.

Body

Triceratops was nine feet tall from its toes to its hips.

Its wide belly was shaped like a barrel.

Triceratops was as long as a school bus.

It weighed as much as an elephant.

Enemies

T. rex was the enemy of *Triceratops*.

A hungry *T. rex* could kill a baby or young *Triceratops*.

A grown *Triceratops* could stab a *T. rex* with its horns.

Three or four *Triceratops* could form a circle to protect a baby from *T. rex*.

T. rex

frill

Babies

Just like all dinosaurs, *Triceratops* hatched from an egg.

The smallest baby skull found so far is about 15 inches long.

The skull had a short frill. It had tiny little bumps over the eyes.

When the baby grew up, these bumps became long horns.

Home

Triceratops lived on muddy flat land near slow rivers. The rivers ran to a shallow sea near their home.

The world was much warmer than it is today.

Triceratops were shaded by very tall redwood trees. Flowers made the land colorful.

Triceratops Was Not Alone

Triceratops lived with other plant-eating dinosaurs.
Edmontosaurus walked on two legs.
Ankylosaurus had a bony club at the end of its tail.
Fish swam in rivers and lakes.
Turtles sat on the sunny shores.
Crocodiles snapped at anything that moved by.
Birds flew in the sky.
Possums scurried about looking for bugs.

Where on Earth?

Torosaurus

Chasmosaurus

Triceratops lived between 68 and 65 million years ago. It was one of the most common dinosaurs. Its **fossils** have been found in Wyoming, Colorado, Montana, South Dakota, and Canada.

Just as you may have cousins and other relatives, *Triceratops* had relatives, too! The dinosaurs looked a lot alike. They all had triangular heads with thin beaks. They had wide crests at the back of the head. *Torosaurus* came from Montana. *Chasmosaurus* came from Alberta, Canada.

Learn More

Books

Dixon, Dougal. *Amazing Dinosaurs*. Honesdale, Penn.: Boyds Mill Press, Inc., 2007.

Landau, Elaine. *Triceratops*. New York: Children's Press, 2007.

Stewart, Melissa. *My First Time for Learning Dinosaurs*. Lincolnwood, Ill.: Publications International, Ltd., 2007.

Web Sites

Enchanted Learning.
Zoom Dinosaurs.
http://www.enchantedlearning.com/subjects/dinosaurs/

The Natural History Museum.
Dino Directory.
http://kidsdinos.com/

INDEX

For Jonah Emile

Bailey Books, an imprint of Enslow Publishers, Inc.

Library of Congress Cataloging-in-Publication Data

Dodson, Peter.
Triceratops up close : horned dinosaur / Peter Dodson.
p. cm. — (Zoom in on dinosaurs!)
Summary: "Gives young readers an up-close look at Triceratops and how its features helped it live"—Provided by publisher.
Includes bibliographical references and index.
ISBN 978-0-7660-3335-1
1. Triceratops—Juvenile literature. I. Title.
QE862.O65.D644 2011
567.915'8—dc22 2009012287

Printed in the United States of America

042010 Lake Book Manufacturing, Inc., Melrose Park, IL

10 9 8 7 6 5 4 3 2 1

Illustration Credits: © Bob Walters and Erin M. Cobb

Cover Illustration: © Bob Walters and Erin M. Cobb

To Our Readers: We have done our best to make sure all Intern Addresses in this book were active and appropriate when we went to pre However, the author and the publisher have no control over and assume liability for the material available on those Internet sites or on other W sites they may link to. Any comments or suggestions can be sent by e-mail comments@enslow.com or to the address on the back cover.

Enslow Publishers, Inc., is committed to printing our books on recycl paper. The paper in every book contains 10% to 30% post-consumer was (PCW). The cover board on the outside of each book contains 100% PCV Our goal is to do our part to help young people and the environment too!

Note to Parents and Teachers: The *Zoom In on Dinosaurs!* series supports t National Science Education Standards for K–4 science. The Words to Kno section introduces subject-specific vocabulary words, including pronunciati and definitions. Early readers may need help with these new words.

Allan A. De Fina, PhD
Series Literacy Consultant
Dean, College of Education
Professor of Literacy Education
New Jersey City University
Past President of the New Jersey Reading Association

Philip J. Currie, PhD
Series Science Consulta
Professor of Dinosaur Paleob
University of Alberta
Edmonton, Alberta
Canada

Bailey Books
an imprint of
Enslow Publishers, Inc.
40 Industrial Road
Box 398
Berkeley Heights, NJ 07922
USA
http://www.enslow.com